Ethereal Serenades in Deep Waters

In the hush beneath the waves,
Where shadows dance and shimmer glows,
The melodies of dreams arise,
In whispers soft as night's repose.

Beneath the moon's pale silver glow,
The sirens sing their ancient lines,
With notes entwined like seaweed strands,
That cradle hearts where magic shines.

Glimmers of fish weave tales untold,
As currents murmur secrets sweet,
Each echo shapes the tales we hold,
In hidden depths where sorrows meet.

The water's breath a soft refrain,
In swirls of light, the world imbued,
With whispers safe from harsh disdain,
In tides of love and dreams renewed.

So close your eyes and drift away,
To realms where time begins to bend,
In deep waters where night holds sway,
To find the peace that knows no end.

The Enchantment of Coral Nocturnes

Beneath the coral's vibrant sigh,
A world awakens, rich and bright,
Where gentle waves roll softly by,
And stars reflect in endless night.

The fish in colors bold and bright,
Trace patterns on the ocean's skin,
A dance of light, a woven sight,
In rhythmic songs where dreams begin.

The sea anemones sway and twirl,
In harmony with the ebb and flow,
Each ocean beat, a precious pearl,
A tapestry that weaves the glow.

And in the twilight's velvet hand,
The whispers of the deep implore,
For every heart to understand,
The magic that the currents store.

So let your spirit chase the tide,
And feel the pulse of night's embrace,
For in these depths, the soul's a guide,
To realms of peace, a sacred space.

Aetherial Drifts Through Luminous Waters

In fields of blue, where silence reigns,
Aetherial drifts like softest breath,
Each current carries magic's chains,
Through shimmering paths of life and death.

The moonbeams dance on water's face,
While whispers swell, a soothing balm,
In tranquil depths, a vibrant grace,
That keeps the spirit wrapped in calm.

With every ripple, dreams emerge,
As distant echoes softly call,
A symphony where hearts converge,
In oceans vast, we rise and fall.

The stars above begin to fade,
Yet lantern fish ignite the dark,
In coral realms, we are remade,
As spirits soar and visions spark.

So drift along the aether's stream,
And let the tides of wonder flow,
For in these depths, we find our dream,
As luminous waters start to glow.

Choral Symphonies from Ocean Depths

From caverns deep where shadows creep,
A choral symphony resounds,
With every note, a promise keeps,
The secrets wrapped in ocean's bounds.

The haunting calls of whales in song,
Bring tales of love and timeless grace,
In harmony where we belong,
In depths where dreams begin to lace.

The rippling sound of distant waves,
A gentle call to hearts in quest,
Where every soul that wanders saves,
A piece of joy, a moment blessed.

As currents weave their magic thread,
And every breath swells with delight,
The ocean's heart serves as our bed,
In choral hymns that chase the night.

So let the symphony enfold,
In sea's embrace, we rise and blend,
With melodies that never grow old,
In ocean depths, we find our end.

Whispers of the Ocean's Heart

Beneath the waves, a secret sleeps,
Where coral dreams and silence keeps.
A song of tides, a gentle grace,
The ocean's heart, a hidden place.

Whispers rise with the foamy spray,
Each note a call from far away.
The stars above, their watchful eyes,
Reflect the tales where magic lies.

In rippling currents, stories dance,
Of ancient ships and lost romance.
They swirl and twirl in salty air,
A melody beyond compare.

Echoes linger, soft and sweet,
In every wave, a pulse, a beat.
The heart of water, vast and wide,
Holds all the dreams of those who glide.

Oh listen close, the ocean's call,
For in its depths, we find our all.
A treasure trove, a gift to share,
The whispers weave a timeless prayer.

Harmonies of Sunlit Waves

When dawn awakens with golden rays,
The ocean hums, its dance conveys.
Each wave that breaks, a note of light,
In harmonies that spark delight.

The gulls take flight, their laughter high,
While sunbeams twinkle in the sky.
A symphony of day's embrace,
In every ripple, joy finds space.

Adventure calls from sandy shores,
As heartbeats match the ocean's roars.
With every splash, a tale is spun,
Of daring dreams and races run.

The tides align, in rhythm sway,
As sailors chart their hopeful way.
Through tempest fierce or calm serene,
The waves compose what must be seen.

So heed the call of sunlit streams,
For in their depths lie tangled dreams.
In every crest, let spirits soar,
Harmonies of waves forever roar.

Secrets of the Sunken Melody

Down where the shadows softly creep,
Lie secrets dark, in silence deep.
The sunken melody, lost and faint,
Whispers truths the sea did paint.

In ghostly halls of drowned delight,
Old sailors' songs take flight by night.
Each swell a memory, each tide a tale,
Of sunken ships and their enduring sail.

Through kelp and stone, the echoes glide,
In murky depths where dreams abide.
The symphony of ages old,
Wrapped in seashells, purest gold.

Where creatures dance beneath the foam,
And ancient spirits find their home.
In every whisper, every sigh,
The ocean's heart is never shy.

So dive deep down, where secrets lie,
And find the songs that never die.
Embrace the calm of waters vast,
For every melody holds the past.

Lullabies from the Coral Depths

In coral beds where whispers weave,
The lullabies of oceans breathe.
A soothing sound, both soft and deep,
To cradle all the world to sleep.

With every ebb, a tender sigh,
As shimmering fish dance bye and bye.
The twilight glows, a tranquil beam,
While waters murmur like a dream.

Beneath the moon, the sea's embrace,
Caresses night with gentle grace.
These lullabies in silver light,
Invite the stars to join the night.

So close your eyes and hear the calls,
Of ocean's love, as darkness falls.
The sweet refrain of waves and tide,
A tranquil song where dreams reside.

In coral depths, let worries cease,
For in the sea, we find our peace.
With every note, the heart ignites,
Lullabies, in moonlit nights.

Mesmeric Currents of the Abyss

In depths where shadows softly wane,
The whispers called from waters deep.
An echo of an age-old pain,
Where secrets in the darkness creep.

The currents swirl like dizzy dreams,
With glimmers caught in starlit eyes.
A song that flows in silent streams,
Beneath the waves, where silence lies.

What horrors hide in ancient tombs?
What memories lie locked in chains?
Each ripple tells of haunting glooms,
Of sorrow carved in liquid veins.

Yet every wave bears tales untold,
Of ships that sailed the tempest's breath.
Of treasures lost, of glories bold,
And hearts that danced with fleeting death.

Ode to the deep, a timeless waltz,
A melody of fate's cruel jest.
In oceans vast, the truth exalts,
The haunting song of life's great quest.

The Secrets of Celestial Tides

Beneath the glow of silver moons,
Where stars are stitched in night's embrace,
The tides unveil their ancient tunes,
A cosmic dance in endless space.

Each wave a tale of time and fate,
Whispering dreams of worlds unseen.
They craft a symphony, ornate,
Of love, of loss, in realms between.

In every swell, a story lies,
Of lovers lost and journeys far.
The heavens weave their soft goodbyes,
As comets trace a dance with stars.

The ocean's heart beats wild and true,
In rhythm with the evening light.
With every surge, it gives its view,
Of secrets held from mortal sight.

So sail upon the silver waves,
Let stardust guide your restless flight.
For in the tides, the cosmos craves,
To share its magic through the night.

Floating Whispers in Fluid Realms

In realms where water's gentle sighs,
Are woven soft with twilight's hue,
The whispers float, as dreams arise,
A delicate dance of hope anew.

In crystal pools, reflections gleam,
With murmurs sweet from lips of lore.
Each ripple holds a fleeting dream,
That calls the brave to seek for more.

The currents curl, a lover's embrace,
With secrets held in soft caress.
Beneath the surface, time and space,
Converge to weave their mysteries.

A symphony of softest tones,
The water flows with ancient grace.
In its embrace, the heart atones,
For fears that haunt this mortal place.

So take a step into the deep,
Let whispers guide your questing heart.
For in the waters, dreams can leap,
And worlds can bloom where once was dark.

The Dreamweaver's Pulse

Through shadows thick where nightmares play,
A thread of light begins to weave.
In every heart, a whispered sway,
The pulse of dreams we dare believe.

Each tangled thought, like silken strands,
Embrace the fears that haunt our nights.
The Dreamweaver calls with gentle hands,
To guide us through our inner fights.

With every heartbeat, stories rise,
A tapestry of hopes and fears.
In colors bold, the truth complies,
As laughter mingles with our tears.

The dreamscape stirs; its magic flows,
Inviting all to take their part.
For in the light where wonder grows,
Awaits the longing heart's sweet art.

So close your eyes and journey deep,
Into the realms where dreams can be.
For in the pulse of night, we leap,
And find the truths that set us free.

Moonlit Currents of Enchantment

Beneath the silver glow of night,
The waves dance gently, pure delight.
Whispers of magic fill the air,
As secrets drift without a care.

The moon reflects on ocean's tide,
Where dreams and wishes softly glide.
Each ripple sings a tale of old,
Of treasures lost and gems of gold.

A figure glides through liquid light,
With silver hair that shimmers bright.
A guardian of the deep's embrace,
In her eyes, the stars find their place.

The currents swirl in mystic flight,
Guiding the hearts that seek their light.
In every splash, a world anew,
Where wonder stirs, and spirits flew.

As dawn approaches, shadows flee,
The magic lingers, wild and free.
In moonlit currents, dreams will stay,
Calling us back, come what may.

Chants of the Aqua Stars

In the depths where silence sighs,
Aqua stars in velvet skies.
They gleam and twinkle, soft and bright,
Casting spells of pure delight.

Each ripple carries a melody,
A secret tune from sea to sea.
The ocean hums, a lullaby,
Inviting dreams to drift and fly.

O gentle waves, an endless song,
In your embrace, we all belong.
The tides, they dance, an age-old waltz,
In the rhythm, no one faults.

With every splash, a story told,
Of pirate treasures, legends bold.
The water sings, a siren's call,
To every heart, both great and small.

As dusk descends, the chorus grows,
A symphony the ocean knows.
In unity, the stars will gleam,
In aqua dreams, we find our theme.

Breath of the Celestial Waters

From depths unseen, a whisper flows,
Through azure avenues, it goes.
Celestial breath on skin so fair,
A touch of magic in the air.

Beneath the waves, worlds intertwine,
In shimmering light, the fates align.
Soft serenades, the waters weave,
Invoking wonder to believe.

With coral reefs that paint the sea,
An artistry of jubilee.
Each sea creature, a note of grace,
In nature's hymn, we find our place.

The call of tides, a soft embrace,
In every journey, we must trace.
These waters hold the keys to dreams,
In liquid realms, all hope redeems.

As twilight falls upon the shore,
We find the echoes of our lore.
The breath of waters, strong and pure,
In celestial sway, we shall endure.

Anemone's Gentle Caress

In gardens deep where colors blend,
The anemone will softly bend.
A tender touch beneath the waves,
In gentle sways, the ocean saves.

With petals bright, like painted glass,
They dance with grace as currents pass.
Their beauty calls the curious near,
In every bloom, a hidden tear.

The sea embraces, warm and kind,
Whispering secrets, heart aligned.
In twilight's glow, they gently weave,
A tapestry that won't deceive.

Each anemone, a story spun,
Of love that's lost and battles won.
In their arms, the ocean's sighs,
A lullaby that never dies.

So let the waters cradle you,
In moments rare, where dreams come true.
For in their fold, we find our place,
In anemone's soft embrace.

Secrets of the Abyssal Lullaby

In shadows deep, where secrets weave,
The tides of silence gently grieve.
Whispers float in currents cold,
Ancient tales of mariners bold.

Echoes sing beneath the waves,
Cradled soft in watery graves.
A lullaby, both soft and sweet,
Calls from depths where dreams retreat.

Stars blink low, in twilight's gaze,
Entranced by depths where darkness plays.
A shimmer in the ocean's breath,
Hints of life and whispers of death.

Hidden worlds in liquid night,
Phantoms dance in ghostly light.
Secrets held in shells and bones,
Murmured soft, the ocean's tones.

Let the waves your sorrows steal,
In the depths, let silence heal.
For in the dark, all dreams remain,
The secrets sing, in joy and pain.

Starlit Waters of the Subtropical Muses

Beneath the stars that twinkle bright,
The ocean sings in pure delight.
Muses frolic on the foam,
Painting dreams where spirits roam.

Dancing in the balmy breeze,
Secrets whispered through the trees.
Their laughter blends with ocean's sigh,
Underneath the vast, high sky.

The water shimmers with a glow,
From silver fish that twist and flow.
Every ripple tells a tale,
Of distant lands and ships that sail.

Cradled in the moon's embrace,
Time drifts softly, leaves no trace.
In starlit waters, hearts alight,
Muses gather through the night.

Awake the dreams that lie beneath,
With every tide and gentle breath.
In subtropical realms, we find,
The echoes of the poet's mind.

Whims of the Ocean's Enchantment

Through whispers of the ocean's spell,
The tides of fortune rise and swell.
A dance of whimsy, bold and free,
Where sky meets sea in harmony.

Frothy waves in laughter's embrace,
Carry thoughts to a wondrous place.
In echoes soft, the secrets bloom,
Unraveling from the ocean's womb.

Shells of gold lie on the shore,
Calling souls to dream once more.
The ocean twirls with playful grace,
In every eddy, leaving trace.

The heartbeats of the tides resound,
With mysteries in its depths found.
Cradled by the ocean's song,
A world reborn where souls belong.

Let whispers of the waves entice,
To frolic in their cool device.
In every whim, a spark ignites,
An enchantment woven in the nights.

Silhouette of the Aquatic Dreamer

In depths where light and shadow play,
A silhouette drifts, night and day.
With dreams entwined in liquid lace,
The ocean cradles this sacred space.

Beneath the waves, where time stands still,
The dreamer's heart, a quiet thrill.
Fish swim by in ghostly ballet,
An aquatic dance in sublime array.

Hushed whispers ripple through the dark,
Sparking life with a gentle spark.
Waves unfold like silk and sigh,
As night descends from the velvet sky.

Every current sings a tune,
In rhythm with the silver moon.
Seafoam curls around the dream,
Creating worlds where spirits gleam.

The silhouette in water wakes,
In watery trails, the starlight shakes.
Let the ocean's magic soar,
For in its depths, our hearts explore.

Fables from the Abyssal Chorus

In shadows deep where whispers play,
A tale unfolds of night and day.
Creatures dwell in waters cold,
Their secrets wrapped in stories old.

With scales that shimmer, voices rise,
A harmony that mystifies.
The echoes dance from wave to beam,
A chorus sings of every dream.

Beneath the tide, their wishes flow,
In currents wild, through long ago.
They weave the fables, cast their net,
In realms where time and truth forget.

A siren's laugh, a shadow's wail,
The tempest's cry, the silent veil.
All woven tight in ocean's lore,
The fables call for evermore.

So listen close, for tales shall bloom,
From depths where light can scarce resume.
In every wave, a world concealed,
Of joy and sorrow, love revealed.

Silken Currents of Enchantment

In twilight's grasp, where dreamers float,
A river runs in a silken coat.
Glimmers dance on threads of fate,
Enchantments weave, they mesmerate.

With every bend, a secret spun,
The waters murmur, tales begun.
A spell is cast with every sigh,
As stars cascade from velvet sky.

In twilight gardens, shadows creep,
While ancient whispers softly seep.
The heart of magic flows like streams,
Awake in depths of boundless dreams.

With gentle ripples, fears abate,
While fairies dance in webs of fate.
Beneath the surface, calm and clear,
The currents carry hope and fear.

So close your eyes to find it there,
This liquid song, this woven prayer.
In silken hues of sapphire night,
Embrace the currents, feel their light.

Serenades of the Hidden Caverns

In caverns dark where echoes dwell,
The earth holds secrets, tales to tell.
A lullaby of stone and night,
Serenades born from ancient light.

With every step, the shadows hum,
Their voices rich, like distant drum.
A waltz of time in tunnels worn,
In hidden hearts, new life is born.

The stalactites like chandeliers,
Reflect the dreams of long lost years.
A symphony of breath and stone,
In every note, a world alone.

Within these walls, the past awakes,
With every whisper, history makes.
The caverns breathe with tales profound,
In every crevice, magic found.

So wander deep, and let them share,
The serenades that fill the air.
In hidden paths, let wonders flow,
And find the beauty down below.

Glimmering Crystals of the Deep Beyond

In realms of darkness, bright and bold,
Glimmering crystals, tales unfold.
They pulse with life, they shimmer bright,
A beacon shining through the night.

Each facet holds a story dear,
Of lost horizons, spoken clear.
They catch the dreams that slip away,
In twilight's grasp, they long to stay.

The depths of time, they guard with grace,
A treasure trove in time and space.
With colors deep, they sparkle true,
Like starlit skies in oceans blue.

In ancient whispers, truths align,
Within these gems, the stars entwine.
A dance of fate in crystal hues,
In every shard, a path to choose.

So seek the glimmer, heed the call,
For in the depths, there lies it all.
With every crystal shining bright,
Find hope anew, and face the night.

Dreams of the Serpent's Song

In the shadows where whispers roam,
Beneath the surface of thoughts unknown.
A serpent's song, both sweet and sly,
Calls to the hearts that dare to fly.

Beneath the stars, in silken night,
Promises whisper, gleam with light.
In dreams, the serpent sways and spins,
With tales of losses, and where love begins.

Through sighs and laughs in tangled woods,
She weaves a magic understood.
But tread with care, for shadows creep,
In dreams of the serpent, secrets keep.

With scales that shimmer, truths unfold,
Of ancient tales, long forgotten, told.
Her voice a melody, soft yet strong,
Guiding the lost, where they belong.

In the twilight where waters gleam,
The serpent sings a haunting theme.
So, close your eyes and take a chance,
To dance with fate in a mystic trance.

Echoes in the Tidal Veil

Whispers flow where the sea meets land,
In the folds of time, by nature's hand.
Tides roll in with an ancient grace,
Echoes ripple, in a secret place.

The moonlight dances on the waves,
As hearts awaken to what it craves.
The ocean's heart beats in time,
With dreams of sailors lost in rhyme.

Shells like treasures, secrets confide,
In the depths where memories abide.
Each wave a story, each crest a sigh,
A symphony sung by the salty sky.

In the hush of dusk, the echoes swell,
Of distant ships and their longing knell.
The briny music of love's refrain,
Calls to the wanderers caught in the rain.

As tides retreat, they leave behind,
Whispers of love, forever entwined.
In the cradle of the ocean's embrace,
The echoes of time find their place.

Serenade of the Shimmering Deep

In the depths where shadows dwell,
Bubbles rise with secrets to tell.
The shimmer calls, a song of light,
Inviting dreams all through the night.

Dancers sway in the water's glow,
Carried by rhythms only they know.
A serenade of the shimmering deep,
Where mysteries promise to keep.

Silvery fins flash like stars,
Guiding the lost and healing their scars.
In currents swift, love's whispers blend,
Through the embrace of a watery friend.

The coral blooms, alive and bright,
In gardens hidden from day and light.
Each petal shines with stories bold,
Of treasures waiting, yet untold.

As darkness falls and silence wraps,
The ocean hums in soft, gentle laps.
A serenade that swells so deep,
In the heart of the sea, where dreams can leap.

The Siren's Hidden Lament

Beneath the waves her voice does weave,
A sorrowful tale that none believe.
The siren's song, both sweet and grave,
Calls to the strong, yet many do waive.

In moonlit waters, she mourns alone,
For hearts that sailed, but never returned home.
Her melody swells with a haunting glow,
Of love and loss in the ebb and flow.

In seashells whispered, her echoes stay,
A constant reminder of dreams gone astray.
With every wave, her tears do blend,
A hidden lament that will never end.

In the depths where shadows embrace,
She sings of longing, of love's embrace.
A song of hope, yet a warning clear,
For those who dabble, in waters unclear.

So heed the siren, with an open heart,
For hidden tales can tear souls apart.
In her lament, find your way back,
Upon the tides that never lack.

Riddles of the Undersea Fable

In the depths where shadows dwell,
Whispers of ancient tales do swell.
Seashells holding secrets tight,
Bubbles rise in the dimming light.

Mermaids dance with silver scales,
Echoing soft, forgotten wails.
A shipwreck's ghost, a story told,
Of treasures lost and heroes bold.

Coral gardens bloom and sway,
While the moon casts dreams at play.
Beware the kraken's playful lure,
For many seek, but few return sure.

Dolphins leap with grace and glee,
Guiding hearts through mystery.
They tell of storms and calm reprieves,
And inked maps on tattered leaves.

So dive within the tale's embrace,
Find meaning in the ocean's grace.
For every riddle wrapped in foam,
Holds a piece of every home.

Twilight's Ethereal Songscape

As twilight weaves its gentle thread,
A tapestry where dreams are spread.
Stars awaken, shyly bright,
Humming softly through the night.

Luna's glow spills silver beams,
Lighting up the world of dreams.
Whispered hopes and wishes sent,
In this calm, where time is spent.

Nightingales sing, their voices pure,
Carrying secrets, soft and sure.
In every note, hearts intertwine,
A melody both sweet and fine.

Clouds drift lazily in the skies,
Painting thoughts with lullabies.
The world enchanted, holds its breath,
In twilight's arms, we taste life's depth.

So linger long where shadows play,
In twilight's grasp, we find our way.
For every song that fills the air,
Is a wish spun from twilight's care.

Tales of the Silken Currents

In streams of silk, the stories flow,
Carried by currents where dreams bestow.
Every ripple sings a song,
Of journeys taken, right and wrong.

Beneath the willows, secrets hide,
Where memories linger, joy and pride.
Fluttering leaves, whispers revive,
Tales of the brave who dared to strive.

Glistening raindrops fall like pearls,
Each one holds the dance of worlds.
With every splash, a laugh ignites,
In the tapestry of starry nights.

Moonlight kisses waters still,
And deep within, time seems to thrill.
Among the currents, softly spun,
Stories breathe, and lives are won.

So listen close, the waters speak,
Of dreams fulfilled and hearts unique.
In silken currents, joy prevails,
And life unfolds through timeless tales.

Aquatic Serenities Unveiled

Where ocean meets the tranquil shore,
Calm surrounds, an open door.
Footsteps traced in golden sand,
Await the tide, with gentle hand.

Waves caress with rhythmic grace,
A ballet, subdued, takes its place.
Seashells whisper, treasures found,
Nature's symphony, a soothing sound.

With every splash, the heart does soar,
Hope rises high with each fast roar.
The sun, a brush of warm embrace,
Paints joy upon the ocean's face.

Driftwood tales and starfish dreams,
In the silence, wisdom gleams.
Aquatic lullabies softly play,
As night replaces golden day.

So stand and gaze, let worries flee,
In watery depths, find your decree.
For in these murmurs, spirits heal,
Unveiling truths we long to feel.

The Silent Serenade of Distant Shores

Whispers of the waves do call,
Secrets from the ocean's thrall.
Beneath the stars, so pure and bright,
Dreams unfurl in the quiet night.

Ebbing tides cushion the shore,
Carrying tales of days of yore.
Each ripple hums a soft refrain,
Float on air, like subtle rain.

The moon gazes down, so serene,
Lighting paths where few have been.
Echos blend with the salty spray,
As night devours the fleeting day.

Magic dwells in the salt-kissed breeze,
Frolicking through the steadfast trees.
Legends linger in shadows cast,
Memories of times long past.

With every swoon, each gentle sway,
The ocean sings, then drifts away.
In hushed notes, eternal lore,
The serenade forevermore.

Whirling Reflections of Aquatic Joy

Rippling waters dance with glee,
Mirroring echoes, wild and free.
Sun-drenched rays sparkle and shine,
Like laughter skipping on the brine.

Fish dart below, colors collide,
In waltzing spins where dreams abide.
Every splash tells a tale anew,
In the vibrant depths, life breaks through.

Bubbles rise like fleeting thoughts,
In each swish, the joy they brought.
The currents hum a lively tune,
A sonnet born from shimmering June.

Waves twirl and swirl in radiant light,
Chasing shadows, embracing flight.
An underwater world, pure delight,
Crafting wonders, out of sight.

Each crest a chorus, each fall a sigh,
Creating beauty where spirits fly.
For in the depths, the heart finds grace,
In the water's arms, a sacred space.

Songs Carried by the Sea Breeze

Gentle whispers on the wind,
Songs of the sea, where dreams begin.
Carried far on breezes light,
Melodies woven through day and night.

Each note a flutter, a tale to share,
Of sailors lost or lovers' prayer.
The soft breeze curls 'round your ear,
Bringing past voices, fading near.

Clouds may gather, storms may roar,
But the sea song forever soars.
With foamy crests that boldly play,
Nature's chorus, forever in sway.

Starfish listen on the warm sand,
To the timeless tales of ocean's band.
Seagulls join in, their calls align,
In perfect harmony, pure and divine.

With every breath, a story flows,
Carried gently where the wild wind blows.
In the heart of the breeze, there's a vow,
The sea sings on, here and now.

Melodic Drifts of Forgotten Tales

Locked in whispers, the tide retreats,
Revealing treasures where silence beats.
Forgotten stories in shells do wait,
To be spun anew, by fate's own slate.

Conch shells hold the wisdom deep,
Each echoed note, a lullaby to keep.
From the abyss, lost voices rise,
Entwined in echoes, 'neath open skies.

Crashing waves cradle forlorn sighs,
Whispers of dreams that dared to rise.
In the gloaming light of dusk, they gleam,
A tapestry woven from each fading dream.

Time drifts on with a soft embrace,
In every grain, memories trace.
The sea's own heart beats slow and grand,
In melodic drifts, where we stand.

Through shadowed depths, the stories roam,
Seeking out a distant home.
With each sigh of the ocean's breath,
Tales linger on, defying death.

Echoes of the Sapphire Abyss

In depths where shadows weave and play,
A sapphire world sings night and day.
Whispers of currents, secrets untold,
As silver fish dance in waters bold.

Bubbles rise like dreams to break,
Chasing wonders, the heart will wake.
A shimmer of scales, a glimmering glide,
In the abyss, where mysteries hide.

Coral gardens bloom, a painted scene,
Colors vibrant, in blue and green.
Echoes call from an ancient reign,
In this realm, all spirits gain.

Lost ships tell tales beneath the tide,
Their stories wrapped in waves collide.
Crimson barnacles clutch to decay,
While time drifts softly, away, away.

Under the blanket of the moon's embrace,
Life weaves through currents, a wondrous space.
In the heart of the ocean, the whispers dwell,
In every echo, a tale to tell.

Lullabies of the Deep-Sea Dancer

A dancer stirs in the ocean's fold,
With grace that shimmered, a sight so bold.
She twirls in rhythms of a watery song,
Where the depths cradle her all night long.

Her skin adorned with the ocean's hues,
In twilight's embrace, she finds her muse.
Anemones sway to the lullaby's call,
As starfish watch from their coral wall.

She beckons forth the creatures that gleam,
With every flick, she fuels a dream.
Octopuses swirl, in time with her sway,
Through currents they weave, both wild and fey.

Gentle whispers glide through the blue,
A serenade for the night crew.
The sea anemones catch every note,
As the deep sea dances, enchanting the boat.

In shadows cast by the moon's soft light,
They swirl and twirl in the plush twilight.
A ballet of bubbles, a dreamlike trance,
In the heart of the ocean, they waltz and prance.

Dreamscapes of the Ocean's Heart

Beneath the waves where dreams entwine,
A realm exists, both yours and mine.
In velveteen shadows, mysteries loom,
Softly they whisper, in depths, they bloom.

The heart of the ocean pulses bright,
With ships of thought and stars of light.
Each wave a tale of adventure grand,
In silvery ripples, the dreams expand.

Luminous creatures with stories to share,
Glide through the water, a delicate air.
With each gentle current, a saga unfolds,
In the ocean's embrace, the dreamer beholds.

From sunken treasures to cliffs of mist,
In vibrant wonders, the soul cannot resist.
A ballet of visions, where fantasies soar,
In this dreamscape, we long to explore.

When twilight settles, calm and serene,
The heartbeat of oceans reveals its sheen.
Awake in the splendor, dive deep and roam,
In the ocean's heart, we find our home.

Revelations from the Twilit Reef

At twilight's veil, the waters gleam,
Where secrets gather, and shadows dream.
Each coral finger reaches out wide,
In the twilit reef where wonders abide.

The cerulean skies reflect below,
In shimmering waves, where the mysteries flow.
Creatures whisper with voices rare,
As currents carry their tales through the air.

In this hidden cradle, time slips away,
Beneath the silence, new worlds play.
Anemones sway to a lull in the light,
As colors fuse in the approaching night.

Beneath the surface, a world unfurls,
With every ripple, a story whirls.
Twilight's embrace, a whispering thrill,
Holds sacred truths in the ocean's still.

As stars emerge in the blanket of blue,
The reef awakens, revealing its view.
In the gaze of the depths, we learn to believe,
In every revelation the waters conceive.

Sonata of the Velvet Waves

Whispers rise with the setting sun,
The ocean's song, a tale begun.
Velvet waves caress the shore,
In harmony, they seek for more.

Drifting dreams on currents bright,
Echoing softly in the night.
Stars above in splendor gleam,
Painting shadows on the stream.

Seagulls dance on the breeze unfurled,
In this magic, lose the world.
Each crest a note, each trough a sigh,
As the tide gives its lullaby.

Let the water cradle your soul,
As the moon plays its gentle role.
Songs of longing, waves embraced,
In this canvas, time is laced.

Through the depths of azure lore,
Waves unite, forevermore.
In this sonata, hearts are free,
Dancing in the melody.

Harmonic Currents of the Mystical Sea

Beneath the surface, secrets swell,
In shadows deep where magic dwells.
Currents twine in a woven lace,
A serenade, a bright embrace.

Oysters open, pearls aglow,
In symphonies of ebb and flow.
Each wave a whisper, soft and clear,
In the heart of the ocean's sphere.

Mirrored skies reflect the dreams,
Of fishermen and silver beams.
Currents hum a vibrant tune,
Underneath the watchful moon.

With every splash, each gentle rise,
A hymn that echoes through the skies.
The sea knows all, and speaks in flow,
In rhythmic language, ebb and go.

In these depths, all wonders weave,
Stories born, and legends achieve.
A harmonic dance, forever sung,
By the mystical sea, all are young.

Elysian Echoes of Liquid Reverie

Where the horizon kisses the sea,
A reverie blooms, wild and free.
Elysian echoes drift and play,
In the twilight's golden sway.

Whirls of cerulean, dreams entwined,
With every heartbeat, whispers find.
Harmony in the quiet sigh,
As clouds drift lazily in the sky.

Siren songs of solace call,
In gentle waves, the world stands tall.
Liquid memories softly glide,
Through the heart where dreams abide.

The breeze carries stories untold,
Of lovers lost and adventures bold.
In the lap of the ocean's grace,
Time is but a fleeting trace.

Feel the pulse of celestial tides,
In the realm where magic resides.
Elysium found in every crest,
In the liquid dreams, we find our rest.

Rhapsody of the Moonlit Tides

Under moonlight, the sea sparkles bright,
A rhapsody sung in the still of night.
Tides perform with a graceful sweep,
As the world around begins to sleep.

Luminous whispers, a silver dance,
Each wave a chance, each ripple a glance.
The stars twinkle like diamonds cast,
In the spell of the ocean vast.

In the quietude, dreams take flight,
Carried away on the breath of night.
The tides murmur secrets untold,
In this lullaby, hearts are consoled.

Waves frolic and tumble, wild and free,
In this ballet of eternity.
Moonlit magic paints the shore,
Where the sea sings forevermore.

Each ebb and flow, a timeless thread,
Binding souls where legends are bred.
In the rhapsody of the tides so grand,
We feel the pulse of this enchanted land.

Whispers of the Ocean's Veil

In twilight's glow, the waves do sigh,
Secrets held by the sea up high.
A tender breeze, a fleeting glance,
In ocean's grasp, the heart will dance.

Beneath the crest where shadows play,
Mermaids weave their tales each day.
With pearly shells and laughter sweet,
They beckon souls their song to greet.

Among the depths where darkness lies,
A shimmering light, the courage tries.
With every ripple, love unfolds,
In whispered dreams, the heart is bold.

The tides will sway, the secrets kept,
Echoes of joy in waters wept.
From shells they share, their wisdom's plea,
In harmony with the vast, wild sea.

So listen close when night descends,
For ocean's heart, the spirit bends.
Embrace the whispers, heed their call,
For in the end, love conquers all.

Melodies from the Depths

Beneath the waves where silence sings,
The ocean dreams of hidden things.
A gentle hum, the melodies flow,
In deep blue realms where wonders grow.

Echoes of laughter, a distant tune,
Carried by currents beneath the moon.
With every swell, a story bright,
From depths unknown to starry night.

Dancing kelp sways to the sound,
In underwater realms, magic is found.
In shadows cast by glimmering fins,
The song of the sea forever begins.

Tales of the past, of sailors lost,
In every note, we count the cost.
But hope remains in the rippling air,
For in the depths, love's still found there.

So listen closely to the seas,
Hear the whispers in the breeze.
They carry back the moments grand,
Of hearts entwined, a guiding hand.

Songs of the Siren's Embrace

In twilight hours, when light does fade,
The siren sings a serenade.
With ocean's breath, her voice does flow,
A haunting tune that stirs below.

Enchanting heart, she lures the brave,
With tales of love, lost in the wave.
Her song a balm, a tender grace,
A timeless bond in water's embrace.

As midnight's clock begins to chime,
The siren's call transcends through time.
Her melody weaves through the night,
A spell of dreams in silver light.

From rocky shores to ocean wide,
The song of love, with the tides, abide.
Each note a thread, a tale retold,
Of hearts that yearned, of passions bold.

So heed the siren's voice so clear,
For in her song, love draws you near.
In watery depths where truth prevails,
The heart will find its way through veils.

Luminous Echoes in Aquatic Dreams

In shadows deep where the sea lights glow,
Echoes dance in aquatic flow.
With shimmering dreams that softly gleam,
The ocean whispers, or so it seems.

A twilight hue, the stars reflect,
In every wave, new paths connect.
With each rise and fall, a breath of fate,
The currents carry love's sweet weight.

Through coral gardens, colors bright,
In gentle currents, hearts take flight.
With every pulse, the waters sigh,
Luminous echoes beneath the sky.

In twilight's embrace, the secrets glide,
As whispers from the ocean wide.
Each ripple tells a story told,
In dreams where treasures may unfold.

So sail away on waves of blue,
For in the depths, the dreams come true.
In luminous echoes, forever be,
A part of the grand, wild sea.

Dance of the Pearl-White Shadows

In moonlit glades where whispers sigh,
The shadows dance, they're drawing nigh.
With each soft step, a secret kept,
In twilight's arms, where silence wept.

They twirl and glide on silken beams,
As if entwined in woven dreams.
Their laughter drifts, a haunting song,
That stirs the night where hearts belong.

By ancient trees that stretch and sway,
The pearl-white forms lead souls astray.
In shimmered light, the world awakes,
A spell is cast that time forsakes.

Yet with the dawn, the figures fade,
Leaving behind a soft cascade.
Of whispers, dreams, and shadowed grace,
In hearts they linger, a warm embrace.

The Fluid Language of Dreams

In silent realms where thoughts take flight,
A language dances through the night.
With colors bright and shapes that swirl,
Each whisper weaves a vivid world.

The stars will hum their ancient tune,
As thoughts and feelings twist and croon.
In gentle waves, they intertwine,
A cosmic brush, a grand design.

Through veils of mist and liquid light,
The dreams will drift, a wondrous sight.
They shimmer soft like morning dew,
In the heart's gaze, forever true.

To fathom worlds where shadows play,
And time itself may slip away.
With every sigh, a vision gleams,
In the fluid language of dreams.

Awake or sleep, the pulse remains,
A symphony of joy and pains.
In quiet corners, voices hum,
In every dream, we'll find our home.

Harmony in the Depths of Blue

Beneath the waves where spirits dwell,
In depths of blue, there's magic's well.
The creatures dance in rhythm's flow,
A tale of life that whispers low.

Coral blooms with colors bright,
A vibrant dream beneath the light.
In gentle currents, secrets sing,
A harmony that hope will bring.

With every ripple, stories weave,
Of ocean's heart, we dare believe.
In sunlit beams, the shadows twine,
In depths of blue, our souls align.

Each wave that breaks, a soft embrace,
In water's hold, we find our place.
The ebb and flow, a tender kiss,
In ocean's song, we find our bliss.

So dive with me into the sea,
Where dreams and heartbeats blend and free.
In harmony, we'll dance anew,
In every hue of azure blue.

Mystical Refrains of the Abyss

In shadows deep, where few may tread,
The whispers rise from what lies dead.
With eyes that gleam like moonlit streams,
The abyss hums forgotten dreams.

Each note a tale of sorrow spun,
In haunting chords, what's done is done.
The echoes call, a spectral choir,
From depths that flicker with lost fire.

Oft shrouded in the misty veil,
The secrets drift on ocean's gale.
They speak of grief, they speak of grace,
In the silence found, we find our place.

As darkness swirls and gently quakes,
The heart knows well what silence makes.
In mystical refrains, we glean,
The beauty found in the unseen.

So linger not in light alone,
For in the dark, our fears are known.
Embrace the night, let shadows flow,
In the abyss, true magic grows.

Siren's Call in the Tranquil Deep

In the depths where shadows play,
A voice lingers, soft as day,
Whispers weave through the cool blue,
Tales of old, both false and true.

With shimmering scales that glimmer bright,
They beckon sailors through the night.
Lost in dreams, the heart does yearn,
For secrets that the waves discern.

Yet beware the depths so sly,
Where laughter masks a mourning cry.
For every song that stirs the soul,
A price is paid to pay the toll.

Beneath the tides, enchantments stir,
With gentle croons, they softly purr.
In eddies where the currents flow,
A beauty hides, more dark than glow.

When twilight dances on the sea,
And stars above begin to flee,
The call becomes a haunting trance,
A twisted tale of fate and chance.

Nautical Fantasies of Celestial Light

Upon the waves, where dreams do rise,
The moonlight weaves through silver skies.
A ship sails forth, on gilded beams,
Into the realm of whispered dreams.

The sailors hum of distant lands,
Where gilded treasures warm their hands.
With every ripple, hope soars high,
As stardust paints the velvet sky.

In this realm where shadows blend,
A radiant path, yet hard to comprehend.
Each twinkling star, a story spun,
Of lovers lost or battles won.

The waves do laugh, the winds do sigh,
As sunlit visions drift on by.
Each crest a promise, each trough a tear,
The ocean breathes, both far and near.

In nautical dreams, we find our place,
A dance of time, a fleeting grace.
Where every heartbeat matches the tide,
In this bright world, we safely abide.

The Ocean's Silent Festival

Beneath the surface, silence hums,
A festival where no one comes.
Dance of colors, deep and wide,
A world alive where secrets hide.

Corals bloom in vibrant hues,
As creatures glide, they softly muse.
Whispers travel on currents bold,
As stories of the deep unfold.

Anemones sway, a lush embrace,
Each gentle flow, a sacred space.
In shadows cast, the magic swirls,
A stunning gift from ocean pearls.

Festivities of the creatures roam,
In harmony, they find their home.
With every wave, a heartbeat shared,
A festival unseen, yet deeply bared.

Among the twinkling sands that gleam,
A quiet dance, like a waking dream.
For in the depths, all souls unite,
In a grand whisper of the night.

Fluid Echoes of the Siren's Song

In the twilight's glow, a melody flows,
A siren's song, where the ocean knows.
Floating harmonies on the breeze,
Entwined with secrets only waves seize.

Rippling notes through the air do fly,
Drawing hearts with their haunting cry.
A tale of longing, a tale of loss,
Of lovers tethered, souls embossed.

With sapphire eyes and laughter bright,
They lure the dreamers to their night.
In currents deep, their voices weave,
Promises of love that none believe.

Yet every note has a tale to tell,
Of fleeting triumph, or the darkened dwell.
An echo lives beneath the swells,
For every charm, a heart compels.

So heed the call of the distant song,
In ocean's embrace, where you belong.
For in its depths, the truth shall bloom,
A fluid echo that scatters gloom.

Shadows Dancing in the Tidal Light

In twilight's grasp, the shadows sweep,
Where moonlit waves and secrets seep.
They twist and twirl in salty air,
A dance of whispers, light and fair.

Beneath the tide, the stories flow,
Of ancient times and myths we know.
With every splash, a tale unwinds,
In waters deep, where magic finds.

The stars above, they shimmer bright,
Guiding the shadows in their flight.
They weave a quilt of dreams untold,
In shimmering paths of silver gold.

The ocean sighs, a gentle breath,
A lullaby of life and death.
With each wave's crest, a flicker shown,
Of secrets kept and battles grown.

As night enfolds the restless sea,
The shadows dance, forever free.
In harmony with tides they glide,
A ballet of the deep and wide.

Secrets of the Sunken Realm

In the depths where light shall fade,
The whispers of the lost cascade.
A kingdom sleeps beneath the foam,
In coral halls, it finds a home.

Merfolk songs, a haunting sound,
Echoing through the ocean's round.
They tell of treasures carved in stone,
And rulers forged from sea and bone.

Lost ships rest in the silken sand,
Their stories grasped by seaweed's hand.
With every tide, the past awakes,
In dreams adrift, where memory shapes.

Glimmers of gold and jewels rare,
Guarded by creatures that linger there.
The secrets of a world unseen,
Lie cradled in the ocean's sheen.

What mysteries the waters keep,
In tranquil depths, both vast and deep?
A glance reveals the hidden art,
Of life entwined with ocean's heart.

Chants of the Submerged Fantasia

In realms beneath the rippling tide,
A chorus echoes, wild and wide.
The sea embraces every note,
Where dreams and fantasies remote.

Each bubble soft, a song takes wing,
A magical, enchanting thing.
With voices sweet like ocean spray,
They weave enchantments in their play.

The fish dance in a rhythmic trance,
While seahorses join in their prance.
Tales of life in vibrant hues,
Flow in the currents, memories muse.

Corals blush with every sound,
Creating art with joy profound.
In twilight's glow, the chants arise,
A symphony beneath the skies.

To listen close, one might just hear,
The beauty held in waters clear.
In every wave and every swell,
The submerged world casts its spell.

Harmonies of the Celestial Current

Above the tides, the stars align,
Their glimmers echo, bright and fine.
The sea's embrace, a mirror clear,
Reflects the cosmos, far and near.

With every pulse, a harmony,
The ocean sings its melody.
The currents weave, both strong and free,
A song of ages, deep as sea.

The moon, a witness in the night,
Lends silver beams, a soothing light.
In every wave, a story flows,
In whispers soft, the ocean knows.

Gentle swells caress the shore,
While galaxies in silence soar.
A dance of tides and starlit song,
Reminds us all where we belong.

As waters rise and shadows play,
The cosmos joins in grand ballet.
In unity, the sea and sky,
Create a song that will not die.

Twilight's Caress in the Seafoam

As the sun dips low, a gentle kiss,
The waves embrace the shore with bliss.
Colors dance in the fading light,
A tranquil heart, a peaceful night.

Stars awaken in the velvet sky,
Whispers of dreams begin to fly.
Each tide brings secrets from afar,
Echoes of magic, like a distant star.

Seafoam swirls like a child's laugh,
Nature's song, a delicate path.
Here the world feels soft and rare,
In twilight's arms we lose our care.

Moonlight glimmers on liquid glass,
Moments linger, as shadows pass.
A symphony of night unfurls,
In every wave, a tale swirls.

Together we wander, hand in hand,
Through soft whispers of golden sand.
The ocean's heart beats true and sweet,
In twilight's caress, our souls meet.

Notes from the Ocean's Soul

In depths unknown, the ocean sings,
A melody of ancient things.
Secrets hidden in every wave,
A call to the brave, a tale to save.

Drifting hearts in the moonlit glow,
The tides of time pull to and fro.
Each note a story, etched in foam,
A whisper of wanderers far from home.

Coral castles, treasures bright,
Guarded by shadows, kissed by light.
Glistening pearls await the hand,
Of souls that dare to understand.

The ocean's sigh, a soulful tune,
Under the gaze of the watchful moon.
Echoes of joy, echoes of pain,
In every ripple, love remains.

Beneath the surface, worlds collide,
In liquid realms, where dreams abide.
Each tide a chapter, each surge a scroll,
Notes written down from the ocean's soul.

Beneath the Moonlit Mirage

In silver light, a dream takes flight,
Mirages dance through the still of night.
Beneath the stars, shadows weave,
A tapestry of magic to believe.

The sands shift soft, a wizard's hand,
Crafting wonders in this enchanted land.
As moonbeams play on the ocean's crest,
Nature's artwork, truly blessed.

Waves chuckle softly, tales to share,
Of mermaids brushing through the air.
A glimpse of wonder, fleeting, sweet,
In this soft world, where dreams compete.

Walking with whispers, breath held tight,
Each moment blooms in the soft moonlight.
A mirage forms, then slips away,
Yet echoes linger at break of day.

Here in the hush, where time stands still,
A heart finds peace, a soul to fill.
Beneath the moonlit, dreamer's sway,
We find ourselves, in night's ballet.

Whispers of the Enchanted Waters

In the heart of the tide, whispers arise,
Soft voices sing beneath the skies.
Enchanting tales of old and new,
Carried on winds, in vibrant hue.

Ripples carry secrets long concealed,
Of star-crossed lovers and dreams revealed.
The dance of waves, a mystical sight,
Guiding lost ships through the night.

Glistening shells, treasures unfold,
Each one a story yet untold.
With every crest, a breath we take,
In the ocean's soul, there's no mistake.

Gentle lapping at the sandy shore,
Whispers beckon, always wanting more.
Like pixies flitting on a breeze,
The waters echo through the trees.

Enchanted waters, a heart's delight,
In their embrace, we feel so light.
Carried away on tides so free,
In whispered dreams, we long to be.

Luminescent Waters of Mystical Chorus

In depths where secrets softly dwell,
A dance of light casts enchanting spell.
Beneath the waves, the chorus sings,
Of dreams and hopes that evening brings.

The moonlight weaves through bubbling foam,
Where creatures twist and call it home.
Each shimmer holds a timeless tale,
Of love and loss in ocean's veil.

With every pulse, the waters glow,
Like whispered wishes from below.
In luminescent hues, they play,
Guiding lost souls on their way.

Luminous trails in the darkest night,
Dance with shadows, shine so bright.
In this expanse, let worries cease,
Join the waters in their peace.

Embrace the depths, the quiet grace,
Where mysteries linger, time can trace.
Let the mystical chorus stir,
In heart and spirit, softly purr.

Untold Legends from the Deep Sea

Ancient whispers rise from salty blue,
Of sunken phantoms and legends true.
Where ships once sailed with sails of pride,
Now rest in silence, the ocean's tide.

Each wave a tale of gallant hearts,
Of hidden treasures and fractured parts.
The echoes linger in briny gloom,
Wrapped in shadows, a watery tomb.

Mermaids sing of glories lost,
Carried away, no thought of cost.
In deep sea gardens, secrets bloom,
With silken tendrils of ocean's loom.

Histories brushed by currents swift,
Life's precious moments, the ocean's gift.
In depths, we find what time forgot,
Personal dreams in perfect knots.

Explore the legends that run so deep,
In the ocean's arms, the stories keep.
A tapestry formed by years gone by,
As waves recede and the seabirds cry.

The Harmony of Tidal Whispers

In silence found on shores so fair,
The whispers drift upon the air.
Tides of rhythm, a gentle sway,
Guide the spirit through night and day.

With every crash, the heartbeat sings,
Nature's song with its vibrant strings.
The harmony of earth and sea,
Unites in dance, wild and free.

Footprints left on golden sands,
Tell of journeys across vast lands.
Where water meets the shore's embrace,
A moment's peace, a tranquil space.

Listen close, the call is near,
Voices carried, crystal clear.
Through salty spray and morning's dew,
Find love and laughter in all you do.

In every wave, a story flows,
In ebb and tide, the heart still knows.
The harmony of life unfurls,
A symphony of hidden worlds.

Serengeti of the Silent Seas

Beneath the azure, vast and wide,
A serengeti where dreams reside.
Creatures roam beneath the swells,
In this realm where magic dwells.

Ocean's heart beats soft and low,
Each ripple sings, a gentle flow.
Starfish dance on the sandy floor,
In hidden gardens, life's encore.

From coral castles to kelp-filled parks,
Life runs wild, where adventure sparks.
The silent seas, a tapestry grand,
Crafted carefully by nature's hand.

With each whisper, the ocean sighs,
Like lullabies that softly rise.
Here, every shell and stone will teach,
The language of waves, forever preach.

In this wild expanse, wonders glean,
A serengeti of calm serene.
Seek the beauty in depths unseen,
For life in silence reigns supreme.

Mystified Soundscapes Amid the Waves

In whispers soft the ocean sighs,
A melody where secrets lie.
The breeze it carries tales untold,
Of ancient mariners and treasures bold.

Beneath the swell, the echoes weave,
Of hidden worlds and dreams believe.
A symphony of sea's embrace,
Where time stands still in wondrous space.

In swirling depths, the colors blend,
A liquid canvas, realms transcend.
With cada crest, new stories form,
In liquid hearts, where wonders swarm.

The tides they dance, a rhythmic play,
A cosmic ballet that sways and sways.
In every wave, a thought set free,
Of all that's lost beneath the sea.

So listen close, and you may hear,
The sound of dreams from far and near.
For when the waves begin to hum,
The secrets of the deep become.

The Veil of Tranquil Waters

Beneath the glassy, calm expanse,
Where ripples waltz in soft romance.
The world above fades from the eye,
As twilight paints the azure sky.

In quiet depths, the shadows play,
With fleeting fish that dart away.
A tranquil hush envelops all,
As nature whispers, night does call.

The moonlight weaves a silken thread,
A path for dreams where hearts are led.
In this embrace, the spirit soars,
To realms untouched on ocean floors.

Each glimmer speaks of journeys past,
Of hopes and prayers that hold steadfast.
Amid these waters, courage brews,
And in the stillness, peace imbues.

Hold tight the moments, feel the flow,
In tranquil lakes where secrets grow.
For in these depths, a boundless grace,
Awaits the heart in nature's space.

Ballads of the Aquatic Spheres

In caverns deep, the echoes throng,
A chorus rich, a serenade strong.
The dolphins chant a sailor's tune,
'Neath the shimmering light of the moon.

A chant of currents, old as time,
In melodies that gently rhyme.
With every swell, a story flows,
Of ships and storms, of friends and foes.

Coral citadels guard their lore,
While strange creatures dance on the ocean floor.
In every wave, a rhythm lingers,
As nature plays with unseen fingers.

From depths obscure to shores so bright,
The ocean sings through day and night.
In every tide, a song they weave,
For those who dream and those who believe.

So sail away on liquid song,
To where the heart forever belongs.
For in the waters, legends thrive,
In ballads sung, we come alive.

Dreaming Beneath the Surface

In visions blurred by aqueous glass,
A world reborn as moments pass.
The stars above, they twinkle down,
While whispers weave a silver crown.

Each ripple hides a thought's retreat,
Where dreams converge, and ages meet.
In shadows cast by moonlit beams,
The depths unveil our secret dreams.

What fortune lies in ocean's keep,
In dreams we dare, in nights we leap?
To dive beneath the troubled waves,
And find the peace our spirit craves.

The silent sirens softly call,
To depths where thoughts break down the wall.
In stillness, hearts begin to mend,
As time suspends and worries end.

So drift awhile in waters deep,
To gather up the dreams we keep.
For in these depths, we find our voice,
And in the silence, we rejoice.

Currents of the Soulful Ocean

In the embrace of twilight's song,
Where dreams and waters gently throng,
The whispers of the tide unwind,
And secrets of the sea we find.

Beneath the stars, a silken grace,
The moon reflects a silver face,
Each wave a thought that drifts away,
In currents deep where shadows play.

A dolphin leaps, a glimpse of glee,
As tides compose their symphony,
With every swell, a tale is spun,
Of sunlit days and nights undone.

The ocean's heart beats wild and free,
In every surge, a memory,
And as the world begins to sleep,
The restless waves their vigil keep.

So let us wander, hand in hand,
Along the shore of whispering sand,
For in the depths, our souls will blend,
In currents swift, with love to send.

The Timeless Symphony of the Deep

A trumpet call from depths below,
In rhythms soft, the echoes flow,
With harmony of fish and tide,
In concert where the secrets hide.

The coral blooms in vibrant hues,
A painted world, a palette's muse,
As every note from ocean's throat,
Resonates where dreams will float.

The gentle sway of seaweed's dance,
In fluid motions, takes a chance,
While turtles glide through liquid air,
In symphonies beyond compare.

Each drop a note, each wave a chord,
The melody that we adore,
A timeless sound, a ocean's grace,
That time forgets in this sacred place.

So listen close, let silence cease,
And find within the ocean's peace,
For in the symphony so deep,
Are promises that tides will keep.

Muses of the Chanted Waters

On shores where silent echoes dwell,
The water's edge begins to swell,
With murmurs soft as evening falls,
The muses call through crystal walls.

They sing of tales from long ago,
Of ancient ships and ocean's flow,
With every wave their voices rise,
A timeless hymn beneath the skies.

The breeze a brush, the waves a rhyme,
In perfect rhythm, pulse of time,
As stars above begin to blink,
The waters weave and gently think.

Each ripple holds a whispered plea,
In melodies from deep to sea,
A canvas drawn with endless grace,
Where dreams emerge, and fears erase.

So let the muses guide us here,
Through waters wide, without a fear,
For in their chant, we find our soul,
In every tide, we are made whole.

Beneath the Waves of Forgotten Lore

Whispers drift through the ancient deep,
Echoing tales that the ocean keeps.
Coral reefs sigh with secrets untold,
In shimmering hues of azure and gold.

Ghostly ships sail in dreams of the brave,
Lost to the currents, the depths, and the wave.
Legends of sailors who roamed far and wide,
Now find their home where the shadows abide.

Beneath the surface, where time cannot tread,
An orchestra plays for the long-forgotten dead.
With shells as their instruments, they sing sweetly,
Melodies woven through the waters discreetly.

Glimmers of starlight dance in the tide,
As memories linger, too precious to hide.
In the cradle of kelp, their stories lay bound,
Waiting for dreamers to seek them profound.

So delve in the depths, let the current embrace,
The tales of the waters, a wondrous place.
For beneath the waves where the lost ones explore,
Lie the threads of our past, forevermore.

Murmurs from the Coral Canopy

In the realm where the corals entwine,
Soft murmurs rise in a rhythm divine.
Petals of seaweed sway in a dance,
Echoing secrets of a timeless romance.

Bubbles of laughter drift through the brine,
Whispers of fish in a graceful design.
The bustling of crabs with their playful chase,
Creates a soft hum in this magical space.

Sunlight cascades, a golden embrace,
Kissing the waters, a warm, gentle trace.
By swaying anemones, dreams drift and flow,
In the coral's embrace, all worries let go.

Colors unfurl, like a painter's delight,
Creating a canvas that dazzles the sight.
Here, the fins flutter like fluttering wings,
In a world that spins with the joy that it brings.

Dive into the dreams within each gentle wave,
Where the heart finds solace, where the soul can be brave.

For in the coral's embrace, life dances anew,
Murmurs from the depths, ever bright and true.

Celestial Strings of the Deep

Stars flicker softly in the watery night,
Casting their glow with a silvery light.
Strings of the cosmos, they strum the abyss,
Singing to sailors, each note an embossed kiss.

Notes rise like bubbles, they twirl and they soar,
Harmonizing whispers that echo the shore.
Every wave lulls, every current replies,
A symphony playing beneath starry skies.

The heart of the ocean, a vast, singing shell,
Carries the tales that the waters could tell.
Plucked by the tides, each sound drifts along,
In the deep, ancient song, where sea spirits belong.

Bathed in the glow of the moon's soft caress,
Wisdom of ages in each gentle press.
The harmony swells, like a tide's tender touch,
In celestial rhythms, we'll rise and we'll clutch.

A voyage awaits on these strings so profound,
Lost and restored in the music we've found.
For within the deep, where silence may creep,
Lie celestial strings, in the waters they keep.

Tides of Enchanted Melodies

Tides roll in softly, a lullaby's call,
Enchanting the dreams of the sea and us all.
With whispers of magic that kiss the sea foam,
Each wave brings a story, a journey back home.

Shells echo laughter of long-ago days,
Tunes flowing gently through sun-dappled rays.
In the heart of the ocean, where spirits abide,
Melodies twinkle like stars in the tide.

The pull of the moon tugs on hopes and despair,
A serenade sung on the cool evening air.
Mysterious echoes entwine with the breeze,
Carried by currents that dance through the seas.

Reach out to the rhythm that stirs in the sands,
Feel the enchantment that life understands.
In the embrace of the tides, let your heart fly free,
For these melodies dearly hold the essence of thee.

Through ripples and swells, the magic flows bright,
Weaving together the day and the night.
Tides of enchantment, a symphonic embrace,
In the lap of the ocean, we find our true place.

The Language of Briny Whispers

In the hush of the tide's soft embrace,
Secrets of the sea start to trace.
Where mermaids weave tales of joy and woe,
And stars in the depths begin to glow.

Waves murmur songs of days gone past,
Of sailors' dreams and shadows cast.
Whispers float on the salt-kissed breeze,
Enticing souls with tales that tease.

Currents carry the echoes of time,
With rhythms that pulse in a gentle rhyme.
Each droplet, a note in a ballad sung,
A symphony where the heart is young.

Light dances like fairies beneath the blue,
Painting the waters with every hue.
The ocean, a canvas of stories spun,
In the delicate dream where the two worlds run.

So listen closely to the briny sighs,
And let the enchantment rise and rise.
For in the language of waves and foam,
A message awaits, calling us home.

Dreamscapes of Forgotten Shores

On sand where the ancients would tread so lightly,
Lies a tapestry woven with whispers tightly.
Each footprint tells tales of laughter and tears,
Of the solemn march of forgotten years.

The moon spills its silver on tranquil waves,
As the ocean cradles those lost in their caves.
Dreamers wander where the sky meets the sea,
In this ethereal realm, they long to be free.

Seashells gather the secrets of night,
And crabs scuttle shyly from the pale light.
The call of the gulls mingles with sighs,
Revealing the magic where twilight lies.

In the dance of the tides, old memories gleam,
Entwining the past with a lover's dream.
Every whispering wave tells its own lore,
Of shipwrecked hearts longing for shores.

So let us wander this mystical shore,
Where dreams paint the ocean forevermore.
For in the embrace of salt and spray,
We find our solace, we find our way.

The Enchantment of Aquatic Echoes

Under the surface, a world alive,
Where visions of magic and wonder thrive.
Fish flit and flounder in shimmering light,
Echoing laughter that dances in night.

Beneath the waves, an orchestra plays,
The thrum of the ocean in vast, fluid ways.
Every bubble a note, a secret confess,
In the depths, they weave stories of less.

Corals bloom like a painter's delight,
Splashing colors beneath beams so bright.
Fathoms deep, where the moonlight glows,
The heartbeat of water in murmurs flows.

Spirits of sailors who sailed in the mist,
Join the whispers, like a delicate tryst.
They beckon to those who have lost their way,
To follow the echoes where dreams softly sway.

In this realm where the day never ends,
The air is alive with the tales of friends.
Listen closely to the aquatic song,
For in its embrace, we've belonged all along.

Twilight Ballads from the Deep

As twilight descends on the craggy stone,
The ocean awakens in softest tones.
Each wave is a ballad of longing and love,
Whispered to stars that shine high above.

Beneath the horizon, shadows embrace,
Secrets are given soft, steady grace.
The sky blushes pink, as the day meets the night,
While the sea hums a lullaby, heartening flight.

Faint echoes of laughter rise with the tide,
Carried afar on the ebbing glide.
Shells cradle dreams on the silken shore,
And the heart finds its rhythm, forevermore.

In tides that crest with the moons' gentle sway,
Dancers emerge from the depths of the gray.
With each swish and swirl in the shimmering gleam,
They twirl with the twilight, as if in a dream.

Oh, listen as night drapes its velvet cloak,
In the embrace of the waves, let your spirit invoke.
For the ballads of twilight will always be near,
A song of the sea, for all who will hear.

Chimeras in the Moonlit Waters

In shadows deep where secrets dwell,
The chimeras weave their magic spell.
With scales that shimmer, soft as dreams,
They glide through water, or so it seems.

Beneath the gaze of a silver moon,
Their laughter echoes, a haunting tune.
They dance in circles, twirling to be,
In moonlit waters, wild and free.

With eyes like stars and tails of flame,
Each creature there, a whispered name.
They call to those who dare to swim,
Where the light grows soft and the edges dim.

Through rippling tides, they spin and play,
In enchanted pools of blue and gray.
The night unfolds in a soft embrace,
As dreams take form in this sacred space.

And when the dawn begins to break,
The chimeras fade, the waters wake.
Yet still, in hearts, their magic roams,
In every wave, they find their homes.

Enchanted Ebb and Flow

In twilight's grasp, a spell is cast,
The sea whispers secrets of ages past.
Each ebb and flow, a tale unspun,
Of lost loves and battles never won.

The tide rolls in on silken waves,
With frothy whispers, the ocean saves.
A mystical dance of rise and fall,
Each heartbeat echoed, a siren's call.

Crystals glisten on sandy shores,
Guarding dreams of the ocean floors.
They weave through fingers, wet and wild,
A child of the sea, forever reviled.

As night unwraps her velvet cloak,
The water shimmers, the stars evoke.
A lullaby hums from depths unknown,
In every ripple, the world's overgrown.

And while the moon drapes shadows tall,
We listen closely to the ocean's call.
Two lovers lost in the timeless tide,
In enchanted moments where dreams abide.

Immortal Melodies of Aquatic Myths

Among the depths where legends drift,
The songs of mermaids gently lift.
Their voices weave a silken thread,
In watery realms where time has fled.

With every note, a story blooms,
Of ancient ships and sunken tombs.
Of sailors brave and tempests bold,
These melodies, forever told.

The sirens beckon with voices sweet,
Enticing hearts with rhythmic beat.
Their tales entwined in the ocean's roar,
Of love and loss on a distant shore.

In tidal harmonies, darkness fades,
As light and depth in chorus wades.
The myths entwined in waves that rise,
Eternal echoes beneath the skies.

With every crest and trough they glide,
In currents fierce where wonders ride.
An immortal hymn of dreams reborn,
In aquatic realms, the past adorn.

Thus melodies soar in twilight's glow,
Where aquatic myths in harmony flow.
And as the stars embrace the waves,
The ocean's heart, each night, it saves.

Fantasies Danced by the Coral Reefs

In gardens deep, where colors play,
The coral reefs hold night at bay.
With tendrils bright, they twist and weave,
In fantasies that never leave.

Beneath the surface, magic swirls,
As fish in patterns dance and twirl.
Each vibrant hue a tale to tell,
In whispered tones, they cast a spell.

The gentle sway of ocean's breath,
Brings tales of life and watery death.
A ballet timeless in currents' grace,
Where every moment leaves a trace.

With echoes of laughter, soft and sweet,
The coral symphony finds its beat.
Where dreams take flight on fins of gold,
In every color, a story told.

And when the sun dips low and sleeps,
The coral reefs hold secrets deep.
In darkness, they pulse with longing light,
Enchanting souls in the tranquil night.

So venture forth where wonders twine,
In the dance of sea, where spirits shine.
For in each wave and shimmering beam,
Lies the heart of a vibrant dream.